HERE I AM

Richard Giles is the Dean of Philadelphia. He is the author of *Repitching the Tent*, a classic text on the design and ordering of church buildings, *Creating Uncommon Worship* and *How to Be an Anglican*.

HERE I AM

Reflections on the ordained life

Richard Giles

CANTERBURY
PRESS
Norwich

Text © Richard Giles 2006
Illustrations © Bob O'Cathail

First published in 2006 by the Canterbury Press Norwich
(a publishing imprint of Hymns Ancient & Modern Limited,
a registered charity)
9–17 St Alban's Place, London
N1 0NX

www.scm-canterburypress.co.uk

British Library Cataloguing in Publication data

A catalogue record for this book is available
from the British Library

ISBN 1-85311-713-7/ 978-1-85311-713-8

Typeset by Regent Typesetting, London
Printed and bound by
Creative Print and Design, Wales

CONTENTS

For
Hans Küng
presbyter, prophet
and pilot of the Church

The Illustrations

The woodcuts are by Bob O'Cathail and are reproduced by permission of the artist.

This book grew out of an ordination retreat
in December 2004
at the
Wapiti Wilderness Retreat,
Maryland
for those preparing for ordination
in the Diocese of Pennsylvania

And I heard the voice of the Lord saying,
'Whom shall I send, and who will go for us?'
Then I said, 'Here am I! Send me.'

Isaiah 6.8

Thus the Lord used to speak to Moses face to face,
as one speaks to a friend.

Exodus 33.11

Will you come and follow me if I but call your name?
Will you come and follow me and never be the same?

'The Summons', John L. Bell and Graham Maule,
Celebration Hymnal for Everyone, *McCrimmons,*

1994

A better preest, I trowe that nowher noon is.
He waited after no pompe and reverence,
Ne maked him a spyced conscience;
But Cristes lore, and his Apostles twelve,
He taughte, but first followed it hymselve.

*Geoffrey Chaucer, 'The Parson's Tale'
from* The Canterbury Tales

I had stood at the foot of a huge north wall and knew un-
questionably that I could climb it, that I was strong enough and
good enough, and knew as certainly as I had ever known
anything that this is exactly where I should be and what I
should do. It seemed wonderfully irrational and ludicrously
egotistical. It needed no justification, no rationale.

It had to be done, and done well, and nothing more.

Joe Simpson, This Game of Ghosts, *Vintage, 1994*

INTRODUCTION

Archbishop Donald Coggan used to say that there was no finer job on earth than that of a parish priest. If I remember rightly, he didn't use the word 'calling' or 'vocation' in this context. He used a more down-to-earth word because what he was getting at was the incredible truth that those of us commissioned to full-time ordained ministry actually get paid and housed to do what we would give our right arm to do anyway.

No two days are ever the same; no one is breathing down your neck or looking over your shoulder. The presbyter is given immense freedom, but with freedom comes responsibility. The responsibility never to betray those who turn to us, trust in us. The responsibility never to lose the sense of awe and wonder at who we are, and at the possibilities of each day as a priest of the Church of God.

For given into our hands is the wondrous 'cure of souls'; the care and succour of human beings in the most significant area of their lives – their relationship with the Holy One, the Life Force, God.

To be a presbyter of the Church of God requires a sense of adventure grounded in the everyday. Although immersed in the structures of the Church, the priest operates like an agent in the field; it's a job without boundaries. There is no way of telling where, or in whom, you will next meet Jesus in disguise.

This springs from a life of prayer in which daily we deepen our sense of union with God. None of the chapter headings (taken from the Authorized Text of the Ordination Services © The Archbishops' Council of the Church of England, 2000–2006, www.cofe.anglican.org) deals with prayer as a separate issue, for it is assumed, taken as read, that prayer is the foundation of everything we are, and do, as priests.

One of the particular treasures of our Anglican tradition is the discipline of the Daily Office. Morning and Evening Prayer, said with a sprinkling of colleagues and fellow-workers or (if necessary) alone, ensures that we are rooted and grounded simultaneously in the psalms beloved of our Lord, the scriptures, and the ancient tradition of our Church. In reciting the Daily Office we grow into a sense of unity with all our sisters and brothers across the world who, as the planet spins, with us maintain an unceasing hymn of praise and devotion to God.

To remain faithful in the discipline of the Daily Office demands of us, not so much a dance of exaltation, as a steady plod of utter determination. Through this privilege of time set apart for God every day, we shall however be brought to a place where we 'comprehend, with all the saints, what is the breadth and length and height and depth, and . . . know the love of Christ which surpasses all knowledge' (Eph. 3.17). For such a prize it is worth switching off the mobile and making the next appointment wait.

The prayer life of a priest is essential if he or she is going to be someone who 'is', who has won through to that state of being in which we rest in God, healed and forgiven. The priest holds within himself the tension of being and doing, eschewing both self-indulgent spirituality and frantic, pointless activity. She lives the advice of St Ignatius of Loyola: 'Pray as if everything depended on God, and act as if everything depended on you.'

As presbyters we are furthermore called to be 'artists of community', as a wise Jesuit once described the priestly call. We have the supreme privilege of shaping with our hands, our prayer, our proclamation of good news, communities of faith, caravans of pilgrims, who will together discover the love, healing, hope and transformation of life in God's grace.

Pamela Hooks, an activist for the renewal of communities in drug-ridden north Philadelphia (the city that saw 380 murders in 2005) began by creating a space which kids without hope could call home. She took a large room in a broken-down old building, and with the active participation of the young people of the neighbourhood, decorated it in vibrant colours and mosaic tiles the kids made themselves. It was a place where they could hang out, do art, take part in drum classes, participate in theatre. Pamela called it 'the healing room of discovery'.

That's what priests do. We create places where ordinary people can experience the extraordinary, where they can hang out with God. We create 'healing rooms of discovery', or as Walter Brueggemann puts it, 'the most dangerous, hope-filled places in town'.[1]

If we were using religious language, we would say that in such work we are witnessing nothing less than re-creation of humankind by the Spirit of God, 'until all of us come to the unity of the faith and of the knowledge of the Son of God, to maturity, to the measure of the full stature of Christ' (Eph. 4.13).

This work is not for the faint-hearted, the lazy, or for those constantly checking their allowance of time off. The priest is someone willing to work at the process of 'growing into what I am' and to do so without anxiety or self-absorption. It is for those who are learning to be at peace with God and at peace with themselves.

It is for those who remain absolutely fascinated by, and therefore tirelessly interested in, other people, knowing that this fragile and funny stuff called human nature is the raw material of God's ceaseless re-creating.

May the chapters that follow help in some small way to remind us of the joy and privilege of the priestly calling, for as the good archbishop said, there is no job, or calling, or vocation, that can conceivably be any better than this.

Note

1 Walter Brueggemann, Clergy Conference, Hershey, Pennsylvania, 30 November 2005.

I

SERVANTS AND SHEPHERDS

Priests are called to be servants and shepherds among the
people to whom they are sent.
Authorized Text of the Ordination Services

The hired hand runs away because a hired hand does not
care for the sheep.
I am the good shepherd. I know my own and my own
know me.
John 10.13–14

Shepherding, when you think about it, does not give a
positive or politically correct nuance to the work of

caring for the people of God. Sheep are rather silly creatures, prone to run away at the slightest pretext, and not given to meaningful encounter with anyone who tries to approach them. By the same token shepherds can in many societies be a rough and ready lot, hard drinkers, and in need of a considerable makeover before they are ready to appear, tidied up and hair combed, in a crib scene in the parish church.

But no doubt we have been exposed to too many stained glass windows to see straight. Stained glass has exerted, ever since the Victorians rediscovered and revamped it, an unholy influence on generations of Christians gathered beneath its rose-coloured shadows. It has probably been responsible for more bad theology in the Church than all the lousy preachers in history laid end to end.

Certainly that young fresh-faced Northern European who poses in our parish church window with a cuddly and unusually co-operative sheep across his shoulders bears no resemblance to the kind of shepherds Jesus knew, or to the kind we are called to become. The genuine article is a tough and resourceful character, a loner who can live off the land if need be, someone best not meddled with, who keeps his own counsel, likely to respond to any frivolous enquiry with a hard, unyielding stare.

If we take seriously then our Lord's use of the shepherd image, we shall be forced to make some readjustments. Note the vivid colour with which 'shepherd' is contrasted with 'hireling'. This is bad news for the greedy or ambitious, or even for those who would use the word 'career' to speak of the unfolding of their ministry.

'Hireling' is someone on the make, just there for the money, who will make a run for it the moment there is any sign of trouble. Despite the frustrations of a system of stipends in which diligence receives no greater financial reward than idleness, those ordained in the Church of England are blessed with a basic parity of income. We need never lower ourselves by asking at the interview the unseemly question, 'And what is the salary?'

Likewise the polity of the English Church is such that, at least in its better moments, the parish knows that in its priest it does not have a hireling in its employ, to be hired or fired at its bidding, but a pastor who by the conditions of his institution is free enough and secure enough to be a true shepherd of souls. The priest who is not financially beholden to his church council is a shepherd who can talk straight to his flock.

Take note that the shepherd spends a great deal of time alone, out in all weathers, unmindful of others or of creature comforts. He lives literally on the edge, putting his own life at risk, in order that those in his charge might rest secure. At night he lies across the doorway of the sheepfold to ensure the safety of his flock. Nothing will get past him, even if he should perish in the process.

The most obvious clue to our true calling, that will distance us from the hireling, is the ability to stand alone. When you arrive in your first parish, the warmth of the welcome by the people, the readiness of the lay leadership to serve alongside you, the willingness to give you headroom to do your own thing, all this will take you by surprise and give you great heart. Remember that sooner or later the test will come when, having exhausted all other options, you will be required as a true shepherd to stand alone, sometimes utterly alone.

The church council will vote your project down, the faithful churchwarden will say one thing privately and another in public, and the supper invitations will dry up. You will be left standing in an empty hall wondering what on earth you have done in coming to this place.

If you stand firm, it is precisely at *that* moment that you will win your spurs as a true shepherd. The people of God long for courageous leadership but don't always know it. Whatever the vicissitudes of the journey, the whole community of God's faithful – sheep and shepherd – will be mighty glad and very grateful when we are all safely back in the fold, snug and safe. But to get there they will need a fearless loner, with the courage to continue the lonely walk even through those times when no one will give you the time of day.

My wise first vicar used to say, 'A popular priest is a lousy priest', and he was right. Immense courage is needed for this lonely path, but once we become enmeshed in special relationships with this group or that, in friendships within the parish, compromised by assurances given or rash promises made, we will be robbed of our calling to be a true shepherd, and will become the most miserable of men and women.

As always, the words and word pictures of Jesus are not meant to make us religious, but simply happy in our work and at peace with ourselves and with God. We shall never know fulfilment or peace of mind if we fail to live out our calling to the best of our ability, standing apart in order to embrace all without fear or favour.

'Teacher's pet' is not a flattering epithet for a classmate, but neither does it say much for the teacher. A teacher with favourites is unable to assess a class accurately, to discern good and bad in all, to stand aloof when need be. Such a teacher has surrendered her ability to teach. She is compromised and to some extent thereafter will be 'played' by the class.

We need not go out of our way to stand alone, or make a big deal of it. The moment of decision will come soon enough. The 'honeymoon period' enjoyed by any new parish priest is so called because it is intense and comes to an end.

It is of little consequence whether the presenting problem is large or small; the basic issue remains the same. It may be a trivial detail in the first week, e.g. a showdown with the flower arrangers who would reduce the altar table to a flower stand, or it may be a mighty whopper – like 'letting go' (to use that delightful American euphemism) the director of music after months of sabotage from the organ stool.

Like the new teacher in the classroom, who must in the first few minutes establish who is the boss if the class is ever going to become a community of learning, the new parish priest must establish her credentials in the parish as the person appointed and commissioned to be in charge. This is not in order to parade the exercise of power (there's precious little of that to be had!) but to create the kind of community where everyone, not just the people who have run the show for the last 20 years, has a voice and a place in the process of building up the Body of Christ.

We are not talking here about control freaks. The priest who truly shepherds will do it with such a light touch that hardly anyone will notice, and those that do won't try it on again. Good shepherding doesn't require a loud voice, or a hectoring manner, and sometimes it will require only the giving of 'the bad eye' (as they say in Yorkshire) to quell the rebellion or cut out the nonsense.

Serving is not servility but, in the pattern of Christ the Good Shepherd, strong leadership which is firm and fearless and which is concerned only for the welfare of the whole flock, stray sheep and black sheep included. Only service of this kind will develop into the self-emptying love out of which is born a willingness to lay down one's life for the sheep.

Anything less will cause us, when the chips are down, to slink away with the impostor or make a run for it with the hireling. The people given into our care will know the difference, and so will our Lord. 'I know my own and my own know me,' says the greatest shepherd of them all.

2

CO-WORKERS

With their bishop and fellow-ministers
Authorized Text of the Ordination Services

But we beseech you, brethren, to respect those who labour
among you and are over you in the Lord and admonish you,
and to esteem them very highly in love because of their work.
Be at peace among yourselves.
1 Thessalonians 5.12–13

In the long-gone days of black and white TV, those in
Britain who could gather round the flickering screen
were gripped by the weekly series *Gunsmoke*, in which

an embattled US Marshall kept the lid on a lawless town of the Wild West.

His name was Mr Dillon, and he was wise, strong and true, but was always in danger of being upstaged by his faithful Deputy, Chester Goode, an eager young man with a pronounced limp, often to be found putting on the coffee pot when not shoring up the walls of the jail. Chester was always ready for the next hail of bullets from the boys of the Crazy Y ranch who liked nothing better on a Wednesday afternoon than shooting up the town.

When any of us is called to be a presbyter of the Church of God, we should never forget for one moment that we are merely deputies of the bishop; faithful Chesters to his Mr Dillon. Whereas bishops and deacons have an undisputed place and a clear role in the pages of the Christian scriptures, presbyters remain murky and indistinct, stand-ins and workhorses for those above them. Only gradually, as the Church evolved, did the presbyter acquire definition as a distinct order.

Deputies we remain, however, and as such we must be content to make a lot of coffee and shore up many walls. We are the best the Church can manage when the bishop is too busy to show up. Let's not get ideas above our station.

I served for 12 years in a West Yorkshire parish, and

I often think the Church should make part of basic training for all ordinands a spell among the moors and mills, where 'not impressed' is the most common verdict on practically everything. The coal merchant contacted by Alan Bennett, illustrious son of Leeds, responded to a request for further supplies with the words: 'Well, I don't care how celebrated you are, you'll never be a patch on your dad.'[1] That's the way it is in West Yorkshire, and it is a fabulous place for priestly formation.

One way we can get ideas too big for our boots is to bang on about being 'priests'. The designation 'priest' is seductively attractive for its mystique of cultic powers and is immediately translatable into many different cultures and eras of world history. There is a tingle down the spine to be had from thinking of oneself keeping company with the parson whom Chaucer so admired on the road to Canterbury, or with Teilhard de Chardin or Maximilian Kolbe, or even Zechariah, father of John the Baptist. 'You are a priest for ever according to the order of Melchizedech', says Psalm 110, and I remember how, waiting in the wings for ordination, I shamelessly applied to myself those words addressed to the Lord's Anointed, so breathlessly eager was I to be admitted to the sacerdotal elite.

'Priest' is easily understood, is common currency among world religions, and is very useful when the chips are down, whether with hospital security or immigration official. It is just a bit unfortunate that 'priest' is, strictly speaking, unhelpful and inaccurate in the context of the Body that we are ordained to serve. 'Presbyter' speaks more accurately of shared oversight rather than cultic role, and of the emergent Church of the communities of the New Testament.

Sadly, in the 2005 revision of the Ordinal the Church didn't have the courage of its theological convictions. With all our talk of the importance of the baptismal covenant, and of the priesthood that resides in the whole eucharistic assembly, some measure of balance would have been restored had the service been headed 'The Ordination of Presbyters (also called Priests)', rather than the reverse. Admittedly it was over three centuries ago that John Milton wrote, 'new presbyter is but old priest writ large', and yes, here I am spitting in the wind. We can but try.

The last decades of the twentieth century, following the Second Vatican Council, saw a remarkable recovery of the building blocks of the early Christian communities, in which a sense of the Spirit's anointing of the whole people of God was glimpsed like the sun bursting forth between the clouds.

No matter how hard the reactionaries try to stuff the toothpaste back into the tube, the secret is out. The vision of Christ's Church is of a sanctified body of men and women, anointed by the Spirit and equipped for ministry, each with a particular vocation and ministry.

This is not to give houseroom to that Reformation notion of 'the priesthood of all believers' (some kind of clericalist nightmare in which every person is his own pope), but instead to celebrate the New Testament vision of the people of God, gathered for worship and action, who become the 'living stones' of a new kind of temple, and who *together* become 'a holy priesthood', called ' to offer spiritual sacrifices acceptable to God through Jesus Christ' (1 Peter 2.5), replacing the sacrificial priestly caste of the Old Covenant.

To allow room for this heady vision to grow in the hearts and minds of God's faithful, those of us called to model in our persons the priestly life that belongs to the whole body need to be generous in heart, not clutching priesthood tightly to ourselves, for 'you shall be for me a priestly kingdom and a holy nation' (Ex. 19.6). Let us sit lightly to titles and customs suggestive of privilege, so that the whole field, not just a sheltered corner patch, may know the gracious rain of God's life-giving promise. 'Shower, O heavens, from above, and let the skies rain down righteousness' (Isa. 45.8).

Clergy come in different species, and one of the least attractive in plumage (despite its habit of continually puffing out its chest) is the bishop-basher. These creatures seem to spend a lot of time despising or resisting or circumventing those to whose office they so unrelentingly yet covertly aspire. They strut around proudly yet pathetically as they do damage to the Body of Christ.

Wherever it springs up, the instinct to take our bat home the moment the bishop or synod takes some action of which we don't approve, reveals a total inability to grasp the notion of order and authority in the Church, a failure to understand our own Anglican tradition.

We do not defy our bishop's authority, or go in for breakaways and secession. We do not do deals with bishops in the middle of Africa instead of our own, or demand of our bishops that they line up with open hands extended so that the 'tainted' may be identified and shunned. Schism is not our thing because we lack the spiritual arrogance to believe that 'truth' or 'purity' takes precedence over love in the company of followers of Jesus of Nazareth.

In any case we are too busy to waste time getting hung up over the foibles of bishops, or the lack of favour they show us. I am astonished by clergy who have the energy to be *angry* with their bishop (a favourite American pastime it seems). Have they no work to do?

We honour those 'set over us in the Lord' first because we honour the Church that has given both bishop and presbyter this incredible privilege. Any system of appointment or election of bishops will have its drawbacks and produce its misfits, but let us ponder our own 'worthiness' for the offices we hold, lowly though they may be, before we throw stones at others. We honour them also, and 'esteem them very highly in love' because they face an impossible task, but in faithfully attempting it they let the rest of us off the hook. The buck stops with Marshall Dillon, and there are times when the menial tasks of putting on the coffee and shoring up walls seem not such a bad deal.

As well as being bishop's deputies, we are blessed by being part of a whole army of fellow-workers. Dull would he be of soul, as Wordsworth might have said, who is not stirred by being part of a body of diocesan clergy processing in to the Maundy Thursday Chrism Mass under the paternal, watchful eye of their bishop. Even the penchant of Anglican clergy for calf-length albs, ropes tied beneath beer bellies, and lurid stoles proclaiming their person rather than their calling, is not enough to dispel the thrill of such being and belonging.

Although theological college life today is rather a loose-limbed affair, those of us surviving from the 1960s look back to a different and more intense experience of formation. Cuddesdon in the latter days of the late great Robert Runcie's regime was for me a tight-knit community of minor gods, and I never quite got over the privilege of being admitted to its hallowed halls. With its Tractarian discipline of prayer and study, the almost monastic regime produced a tremendous *esprit de corps*. It gave me an extraordinary sense of being enlisted in a unit of God's commandos.

These are different days, and not everyone is such a hopeless romantic, but nevertheless those of us called to serve as presbyters of the Church of God are admitted into a glorious company. Let us never for a moment forget the privilege. Deputies we may be, but what marshals we serve! What magnificient companions has God given us for our journey! We are blessed indeed, and while limping we may be, we walk tall with God's friends.

Note

1 Alan Bennett, *Untold Stories*, London, Faber & Faber, 2005.

3

PROCLAIMING

They are to proclaim the word of the Lord.
Authorized Text of the Ordination Services

The spirit of the Lord God is upon me,
because the Lord has anointed me;
he has sent me to bring good news to the oppressed,
to bind up the broken-hearted,
to proclaim liberty to the captives, and release to the prisoners;
to proclaim the year of the Lord's favour.
Isaiah 61.1–2a

Late in the afternoon of 30 September 1938, Britain's Prime Minister, Neville Chamberlain, flew home from

Munich having braved the monster in his lair. He stepped from his aeroplane at Heston airfield to flourish in front of the assembled reporters a document signed by Herr Hitler and himself, assuring the world that it was the desire of their two nations 'never to go to war with one another ever again'.

It was a document Chamberlain had fought courageously and tenaciously to secure, the fruit of a journey that his contemporaries regarded as 'a startling and audacious innovation',[1] a bold initiative that took his Foreign Secretary's breath away.

Chamberlain deserved a magic moment, and from the steps of a tiny aircraft apparently held together by bits of string, he made a proclamation. His proclamation was of 'peace with honour . . . peace for our time', and our knowledge of subsequent events should not for a moment blind us to the impact of this proclamation on a people desperate for hope of avoiding the yawning abyss of war.

We likewise look out on a people equally desperate. The difference is that, for the most part, people do not realize their need. Their hunger for God is dulled by countless little snacks of spiritual junk food. There are no reporters jostling for position to ask us questions, no phone calls from producers of breakfast shows. Like the prophets of old, we have to make our own waves.

The presbyter of the Church of God has a proclamation to make more akin to a speech at a wedding reception. Everyone is having a good time, and people don't necessarily want to listen to speeches, but if you're the best man that's what you are here to do. You rise, look around you hopefully at the unheeding masses, and with some diffidence strike your fork against your wineglass. Gradually the hubbub fades, a few cry 'Shush!', and people move around in their chairs to look at you expectantly. You're on.

Make no mistake about it, once we are launched into it, we experience, after all the butterflies, a certain thrill from this encounter (all clergy are frustrated actors, are they not?).

As we get better at it, we wait for silence to fall, we look around the room with a sense of authority, we feel the anticipation, and let the seconds tick away as people wait, and wonder. We savour the moment, and only then begin.

The scriptures set before us images of proclamation passive as well as active. The psalmist sings that 'The heavens proclaim his righteousness; and all the peoples behold his glory' (Ps. 97.6), and much of our proclamation will consist of letting God's glory shine through while we remain silent. It will demand that we not get in the way of what speaks for itself of God's presence.

One of the priests who played a part in shaping my own vocation used to say, 'The Mass well said converts more people than many sermons.' I have since come to see how right he was, even though today we would not include fiddle-back chasubles and the Canon recited at breakneck speed as essential accoutrements to a eucharistic celebration.

That acute observer of life, Alan Bennett, standing apart from the regular worship of the Church, describes attending a (Roman) Requiem Mass for a friend, and gets the proclamation of pilgrimage in one go: 'I never understand how they get it over with quite so quickly, Holy Communion in the Anglican service [being] more of a journey.'[2]

Allowing silence to descend upon the assembly of faith gathered to make eucharist, and holding and nurturing that silence; standing around the altar table having ended (rather than interrupted) the Eucharistic Prayer with the burst of praise of the *Sanctus*, hands uplifted; sitting quietly in community after receiving communion, our journey (for the moment) completed, the work of the people of God done; all these are proclamations in the liturgy of God's glory let loose among broken men and women. In such ways do we 'proclaim the Lord's death until he comes' (1 Cor. 11.26).

Proclamation is calling for silence amid the chatter

and frantic business of the world, calling the people to look and see, to touch and savour the saltiness of God's presence in the world. Proclamation is also speaking up when all are silent, is standing alone when those around you have upped and left to take another path.

Waiting for a flight at Calgary Airport recently, I witnessed what appeared to be a nice little piece of proclamation. Our seat in the coffee bar looked through a glass screen into Dante's *Inferno* – the smokers' room. A squad of Canadian Army soldiers in fatigues came in and sat round a table, quiet enough and causing no bother. Suddenly, however, they were transformed into a pack of hungry hyenas, pointing over my shoulder, nudging one another, jeering, faces contorted with empty cruel laughter. I turned to see two other soldiers sitting behind us. One was white, the other black.

I can only guess at the internal politics of that squad, but they didn't look a bed of roses. It seemed clear enough that the white guy sitting behind me had made up his mind not to let the black guy stand alone. He was willing to take the cat calls and the abuse in order to show solidarity with the outcast of his world. Here was proclamation, quiet, determined and costly, which would in the end, by sheer persistence, prevail and change lives.

Active proclamation can require courage also in surroundings far more urbane and civilized than a squad room. I have lost count in my own journey of the times I have come away from committee meetings of the great and the good in which I encountered plain silliness, wrong-headedness or even injustice being propounded by those who should know better, only to despair of myself for not having spoken up. By my silence I had become an accessory to something less than what is true, or honourable, just, or pure.

To give faithful proclamation thus requires constant vigilance, for the loneliness of the long-distance proclaimer lies in the fact that it is among the very people that one most respects and admires that the lone voice often needs to be raised. Once raised, of course, it is often seized upon as the new insight, the new direction, obvious to all with eyes to see. But at the beginning, when one opens one's dry mouth to speak, it is a raw, unthinkable thought, scandalous in its nakedness.

Jesus tells us in no uncertain terms to be bold: 'What I say to you in the dark, tell in the light; and what you hear whispered, proclaim from the housetops' (Matt. 10.27). The soapbox has never been part of the standard Anglican kit, however, and speeches from backs of lorries are rarely the name of the game today (so relax!). Our boldness will consist rather of using the opportunities given us – in the Sunday homily, the newsletter, the comment for the local press, the webpage – with the utmost care, and a real sense of the power placed in our hands. Preparing words for such occasions is not a chore to be got through, but a sacred trust. Every time we ponder the awesome responsibility of these moments, we are getting slowly to our feet, tapping the wineglass for silence, and looking around us, slowly and calmly, and with a bold spirit.

Proclamation will sometimes burst forth from us in the most routine of situations. A couple of years back, my annual report to our diocesan convention on the doings of our cathedral (yawn!) included mention of our vital work with people of other faith traditions, and I was prompted to quote Bishop John Taylor who reminded us (as a good Evangelical) that if interfaith dialogue is ever to become real, it must be a risk-taking business, in which there is as much chance of, let us say, a Christian becoming a Jew, as a Jew becoming a Christian.

Well! Within two days I had received a letter of outrage from one of our few 'biblical' parishes asking me whether our Lord had died in vain on the cross, and I was being targeted in one of those vitriolic websites of the Righteous Right run out of someone's garage in Iowa.

So be it. The attention of the assembly had been gained, and proclamation had been made. All when I least expected it, plodding through the desolate pages of an annual report. So be warned, and be ready.

Notes

1 Iain MacLeod, *Neville Chamberlain*, New York, Atheneum, 1962.
2 Alan Bennett, *Untold Stories*, London, Faber & Faber, 2005.

4

WATCHING

. . . and to watch for the signs of God's new creation.
Authorized Text of the Ordination Services

Be dressed for action and have your lamps lit; be like those
who are waiting for their master to return from the wedding
banquet, so that they may open the door for him as soon as he
knocks.
Luke 12.35–36

'Watch out!' Words shouted or shrieked the split-second
before the cricket ball hits your head, or the scaffolding
plank from six storeys up fells you to the floor. Depend-

ing on the volume or urgency of tone, these two words can cause us either to freeze, or to run for our lives.

These two words spoken slowly and quietly can also reduce us to pulp. A deadly serious warning alerting us to the malice of others intent on doing us harm. 'I would watch out if I were you' is a warning more likely to keep us awake at night than any amount of whizzing cricket balls or falling planks, for the threat comes 'at an hour you least expect'.

The watching required of the presbyters of the Church of God is of a different order, and yet will always include an element of warning. Sometimes we see a member of the community of faith getting themselves into a bigger and bigger mess – in a personal relationship going nowhere, an addiction, or a poisonous resentment – and it becomes our bounden duty to take this person aside and gently but firmly intervene. This may go against the grain of our own inclination, or against received wisdom ('Oh, you must let people make their own way in life. It's not our place to interfere'). Occasionally, however, it just has to be done, because there is no one else talking sense to that person, and because that's part of what we are ordained to do, as 'watchmen of the Lord'.

The image of watchfulness given by our Lord consists not so much of shouting a warning (although that will always be a part of it) as being in a constant state of readiness. Many clergy these days find ourselves responsible for staff management, even on a small scale, and are familiar with the anxious moment when we phone the office (and get the *real* telephone manner of the receptionist) or call back there unannounced to collect a forgotten document. What on earth do we find?

Jesus calls for a transparency in all of us, an honesty in all our dealings with others, that ensures that the work rate, the tone of voice, the attitude to our task, remains exactly the same, whether or not the boss is in earshot. That is why it should always be possible with us to 'shout from the housetops' what is 'whispered in private'. Our calling is to make the two indistinguishable; in our faith communities and in ourselves.

The image of the watchful slaves used by Jesus (Luke 12.35–38) is seminal. First, because we are to see ourselves in the service of God as slaves, rather than as superannuated and unionized employees. We don't have rights, we don't have a career; we simply have the privilege of being who we are by God's grace.

Second, we note that the occasion is not one of dread, but of joy. We do not await in fear and trembling a capricious master liable to thrash the living daylights out of us if the mood so takes him, but a beloved master returning home on the happiest day of his life. He can't wait to get home, and we can't wait to welcome him.

It isn't always party time for watchmen, however. As a boy I well remember the nightwatchman posted alongside road repairs to guard the machines and to keep people from falling into the hole (presumably when the pubs closed). I thought it a rather romantic though lonely job, and rather envied the watchman his little canvas shelter – a bit like a sentry box – and his brazier of hot glowing coals. Even in these high-tech times, security men are still used to patrol the 'sheepfolds' of commercial and industrial enterprises, and our newspapers are full of the brutal treatment they can receive at the hands of criminals should their watchfulness lapse. Watching is no piece of cake.

The words of the Ordinal use an even larger canvas, however. Not just warning, not just protection, but constant watchfulness for 'the signs of God's kingdom in the world'. The presbyter is to be the eyes and ears of the community that longs for God and desires to usher in God's realm.

How can we be watchful for the signs of God's kingdom? By re-imaging ourselves and the call of God's people in terms of the imagery used by our Teacher. Above all, Jesus was concerned to show that 'growth' in terms of the kingdom of God is measured in terms of getting smaller – a delightfully back-to-front notion typical of he who loved to turn things on their head.

Lewis Carroll captures the paradox perfectly in *Alice's Adventures in Wonderland* when he describes how Alice was more than once prevented by her size from going where she wanted to go, or being who she wanted to be, and had to learn what it would take to reduce her stature. Glimpsing through a tiny doorway 'the loveliest garden you ever saw', she finds on a table before her a little bottle with the words '"DRINK ME" beautifully printed on it in large letters'. After appropriate hesitation, Alice drinks, and is rewarded: '"What a curious feeling!" said Alice, "I must be shutting up like a telescope."' Later, trapped in the tiny house of the White Rabbit, she ate the tiny pebbles turned into cakes, and 'began shrinking directly'. She ran from the house, and her adventures in Wonderland continued apace.

God prepares for us also a table (Ps. 23.5) and invites us to drink; of the water that will become in us 'a spring of water gushing up to eternal life' (John 4.14); and from the cup that he himself will drain to its dregs (Matt. 20.22). In consuming these life-giving medicines of God are we brought to an understanding of our true stature. We grow smaller, more humble, more wondrous in our appreciation of the loveliest of gardens into which we are beckoned, the place where our adventures begin.

Smallness is in fact one of the most significant signs of the kingdom of God for which we must be constantly on the alert. The stories that Jesus loved to tell about the kingdom focused more often than not on something small and easily overlooked; the grain of salt, the mustard seed, the pinch of yeast, the tiny pearl, the lost coin. The presbyter of the Church of God is constantly on the lookout for such signs of God's kingdom amid the structures of the Church and the success stories of the world. We shall find these signs in the least likely of places: in the shy little person who will one day be a prophet; the misfit with a gift of healing; the loser who this time really is going to turn his life around; the newest member who speaks most deeply of the things of God.

Reversal is another key sign of the domain of God for which we are to be watching. Jesus delighted in showing us how the last shall be first, the proud shall be humbled, the publican preferred, the poor widow praised, the powerful brought down and the rich sent away empty.

This task of throwing a spanner in the works of the world's sense of order and priority is a godly calling, and one for which the first followers of Jesus were renowned and feared. 'See, they have turned the whole world upside down' (Acts 17.6). And now the mantle of Elijah has fallen on Elisha, i.e. on you and me. Now it is our turn to shake up the world.

To be a faithful watchman we need above all the gift of what the Buddhist tradition describes as 'mindfulness' in which we are so awake, alert, and focused that we miss nothing. 'In Buddhism,' writes Thich Nhat Hanh, 'our effort is to practise mindfulness in each moment – to know what is going on within and all around us . . . mindfulness is very much like the Holy Spirit. Both are agents of healing.'[1] Every raindrop on a leaf becomes in itself a whole world to us. Nothing is inconsequential, nothing unworthy, nothing irredeemable. Everything contains the infinite potential and mind-blowing beauty of God's constantly unfolding creation.

'Stay awake' (Matt. 26.41) was our Lord's plea to his far from attentive disciples in Gethsemane. They were at that time poor watchmen, more adept at huddling in a corner of the fold rather than lying across the doorway, more interested in their own seat in heaven than standing alongside their condemned leader. But their time would come, and they quickly learned how to warn and keep safe the flock, and how to turn the world upside down with their courageous insistence that the signs of the domain of God were the true key to the well-being, happiness and peace of the whole world. Now it is our turn to stay awake and keep watch, so that we too may know the reward of the faithful slave when his master returns home:

Blessed are those slaves whom the master finds alert when he comes; truly I tell you, he will fasten his belt and have them sit down to eat, and he will come and serve them.

Luke 12.37

Note

1 Thich Nhat Hanh, *Living Buddha, Living Christ*, New York, Riverhead, 1995.

5

MESSENGERS AND STEWARDS

They are to be messengers, watchmen and stewards of the
Lord; they are to teach and to admonish, to feed and provide
for his family.

Authorized Text of the Ordination Services

Who then is the faithful and prudent manager whom his
master will put in charge of his slaves, to give them their
allowance of food at the proper time? Blessed is that slave
whom the master finds at work when he arrives.

Luke 12.42–43

Being a messenger is, like the curate's egg, good in parts.
Carrying messages is a role we tend to resist: 'Tell him

yourself!' is a natural retort to being asked to pass on other people's news. We somehow consider it beneath us; we are not other people's skivvies. Added to that, the business of carrying messages is a precarious and sometimes short-lived occupation; the history of the message-taking profession makes recruitment a tough prospect. Back when kings were really kings, the bearers of bad tidings were likely to be hacked to pieces for their trouble. Down to our own day, the saying persists: 'Don't shoot the messenger'. It's a dangerous and often misunderstood game.

Being a bearer of good news is, of course, a different story, though subject to its own problems. Arriving back home breathless with excitement at the news we have to share, we may be greeted with 'I know, I just heard!' or, even worse, with a stifled yawn of indifference. As messengers our balloon is easily burst, or our spirits crushed, though occasionally our breaking good news will be matched by an equally excited response, and that will make the good news sweeter still.

Stewarding is likewise not a pushover. The Gospels are full of stories about stewards, some faithful, some bent, but all of whom were at the mercy of the capricious or suddenly returned master who would call them to account. Stewards were responsible for the many-layered larger households of the Mediterranean world of

Jesus' time, and it was a task in which constant vigilance was essential for survival in the job.

Today, 'steward' is a familiar designation on Tyneside and elsewhere in the North of England for the person responsible for a working men's club; it combines the roles of mine genial host with the keeping of balanced books and of law and order. Obviously stewarding has not got any easier over the millennia. As those called to be messengers and stewards, therefore, presbyters of the Church of God are not in for an easy time.

If in doubt about the job description, we have only to look at the story of the Exodus. Moses, despite a decidedly underwhelming enthusiasm for the job, is the archetypal messenger and steward. God tells Moses, 'I will send you to Pharaoh to bring my people, the Israelites, out of Egypt' (Ex. 3.10), but in the face of Moses' persistent excuses, God offers him Aaron, his brother, as mouthpiece and go-between.

The role of Aaron the Levite is peculiarly appropriate as a model for the presbyter. He is not top dog, but is appointed to serve as the necessary voice without which the message of God's chosen instrument will not be heard, and God's people will not be rescued.

Aaron's call is born out of exasperation, for 'the anger of the Lord was kindled against Moses' (Ex. 4.14). God points to Moses' brother Aaron coming to meet him, for when he sees you his heart will be glad'. God goes on to say, 'You shall speak to him and put the words in his mouth; and I will be with your mouth and with his mouth, and will teach you what you shall do. He indeed shall speak for you to the people' (Ex. 4.15–16).

Aaron is a good man and faithful brother. He seeks out Moses and delights to be reunited with him. He is not jealous or resentful, and when the deal is explained is happy to play second fiddle. In many respects – chiefly his fluency – he leaves Moses standing (isn't that often the way with God's call?). Admittedly, Aaron did later take that little wrong turning into golden calf production, but that seems to have been viewed as a moment of madness, and his priestly role continued undiminished.

So then, the presbyter may be thought of as second best, with a role arising from necessity rather than design. We are useful simply because we are there and are not afraid to speak out. We rejoice in our special gifts, and are content to remain in a supportive role.

We delight in the company and service of those set over us in the Lord, quietly aware that they could not perform their role without us. There is no guile or resentment in our heart for not being someone else. We may have wanted to play the lead, and get the Moses part, but are content to be who we are, beloved of God in our own form of service to God's people. We have learned that in any league table it's no bad thing to be tucked in just behind the leader.

The Ordinal makes clear that messengers and stewards have a special responsibility in their words and actions to 'teach and admonish' and to 'feed and provide for' God's family. Teaching and feeding are often much the same thing – at least they are when the teacher is gifted.

My old grammar school in Small Heath, Birmingham, was as about as unfashionable as schools can get. We were co-ed, not boys only; played football, not rugby; we were Birmingham City territory, not the Villa. When anyone got into Oxbridge from our place we all got a day off, so sensational was the feat.

But within those hallowed halls there walked a handful of dedicated and gifted teachers who excited us about the subjects they taught, and opened up horizons far beyond the Coventry Road. They fed as well as taught us. They nurtured us with their own milk, and changed our lives. Mr Davis fostered my love of art and architecture; Miss Haworth my love of maps and travel (I can still hear her voice reminding me that Pennsylvania produces coal and steel); and Mrs Boote taught me that literature is not to be studied, but explored and savoured and devoured. She it was, I like to think, who discerned in me the first inklings of a vocation (perhaps it was the flawed priest of Greene's *The Power and the Glory* that did the trick).

When one of these minor deities expressed their disapproval of or disappointment in us, terrible was that punishment, and it needed only a look. The ability to admonish effectively, to correct a course in order to bring back stability and purpose, is, we recall, a very necessary part of teaching. Its effectiveness, however, arises not from a sadistic love of punishment, but from the teacher's real concern for the pupil, and from a relationship of mutual trust and affection in the context of which admonition is powerful because it is reluctantly given and remorsefully received.

We presbyters of the Church of God have the same opportunity to teach in such a way that we feed and transform the lives of those in our charge. We can all look back on those priests and ministers who both taught and fed us, not just with words but by a way of life. I realize now that my own fate was sealed, long before I realized I had a vocation, by being nurtured as a child at the feet of people like Arthur Beaumont, my gentle, learned and saintly parish priest, and his assistant, Captain Harris of the Church Army.

In this teaching and feeding, tiny incidents will speak to us down the years, long after sermons and lessons are finished and forgotten. I well remember the good captain, standing with me in the churchyard before Evensong, when an eager boy came running up with a full beer bottle he had found in the long grass. The boy somehow managed, accidentally, to drop and smash the bottle, drowning the (teetotaller) captain's feet with Mitchell and Butler's finest ale. 'Oh dear' was the sum total of his rebuke, and I have never forgotten it.

Each of us will have a hero for whom we thank God in this process of teaching and admonishing, feeding and providing for. These exemplars of the Christian Way were not ends in themselves, but were sent to move and incite us to go and do likewise. I pray that the soaking of Captain Harris's feet was not in vain.

6

SEARCHING AND GUIDING

. . . to search for his children in the wilderness of this world's temptations, and to guide them through its confusions.

Authorized Text of the Ordination Services

Today salvation has come to this house, because he too is a son of Abraham. For the Son of Man came to seek out and to save the lost.

Luke 19.9–10

The story of Zacchaeus (Luke 19) may have begun life in our minds as a charming Sunday school story (I seem to recall a particularly appealing colour poster – Elsie Anna

45

Wood perhaps – that was unfurled every time this story came up) but it is much, much more. It encapsulates in a mere ten verses the whole theology of humankind's encounter with God. In particular it captures the mystery of our mutual searching out: we seek God, but God already has his eye open for us, searching the crowd for our face.

If we have ever tried to rendezvous with our spouse in a supermarket, or with a friend outside the ground for a football match, we know only too well that it takes two; a solo search (unless the other stands absolutely still and has spotlights trained on them) is futile. Effective search is a dialogue.

The psalmist cries out, 'O God, you are my God, I seek you, my soul thirsts for you' (Ps. 63.1), and our longing for God is a constant theme of both Hebrew and Christian scriptures. Jesus' words, 'Ask, and it will be given to you; search, and you will find' (Matt. 7.7) provide the response we long to hear. We spend a lot of time thinking how we may best seek God, but at the heart of the three faith traditions of the Abrahamic line is the wondrous truth that it is God who seeks out his beloved ones.

Whether the highly unsuitable Moses at the burning bush, or the shady character Zacchaeus up his sycamore tree, the story is the same; God seeks us out. We do not have to strive and strain to find him, but only to put ourselves in the way of his love. Then the dialogue of our mutual longing can begin. We need only to *want* to be found, in order for us to experience God's seeking us out.

> I fled Him down the nights and down the days;
> I fled Him down the arches of the years.

Thus begins Francis Thompson's famous poem in celebration of the unrelenting footfall of God down the alleyways of our avoidance and subterfuge and contentment with second best. In the moment of final surrender to the seeking-out God, the poet puts these words in the mouth of God (who was evidently at that time heavily into 1662):

> Ah, fondest, blindest, weakest,
> I am He Whom thou seekest!
> Thou dravest love from thee, who dravest Me.
> *Francis Thompson, 'The Hound of Heaven'*

There was no coyness or self-delusion about Zacchaeus. He wanted God and he wanted God bad. He somehow knew that this Jesus of Nazareth, whose parade was about to pass through town that day, was his best chance ever of finding his way back to God. Somehow Zacchaeus had to find a way of putting himself in the way of God's love. This he accomplished by the simple expedient of climbing a tree to get a ringside seat as Jesus passed by.

Thereafter the dialogue could begin: 'Hurry up and come down,' says Jesus, 'for I must stay at your house today.'

The response of Zacchaeus was one of overwhelming joy, and he 'hurried down' in order to make it happen. Furthermore, his words and gestures were fulfilled in deeds: 'Look, half of my possessions, Lord, I will give to the poor; and if I have defrauded anyone of anything, I will pay back four times as much.'

Jesus delights in the straightforwardness and generosity of this former schemer and hoarder, and announces: 'Today salvation has come to this house' (Luke 19.9).

Zacchaeus stood himself in the middle of the stream of God's love in his own moment and his own way. We do it in our own generation by likewise being aware of the opportunities God gives us to greet him as he passes by; to wear our hearts on our sleeves as we jostle to get a glimpse, and to be ready without hesitation or compromise to give God our unqualified and risk-taking response of 'Yes!'

As presbyters of the Church of God we are privileged

to be nothing less than go-betweens in the dialogue of seeking out, between God and humanity. All too aware of our own need of, and longing for, God, we are called to articulate the longing of humankind for God, even in apparent indifference of rejection, and the longing of God for us.

Our knowledge of God's love for humankind does not, however, make us blasé, assuming that everything will finally slot into place for everyone if they rummage around in the world long enough. Rather, we know that intervention is often called for in seeking out the lost. We don't just sit and watch others flounder and perish.

Presbyters of the Church of God are pro-active inter-ventionists in the seeking-out business; the mountain rescue team of God's kingdom. Trained to be ready and alert when we see others attempting feats too difficult for them, ill equipped and unaware of the dangers faced or the lives of others put at risk. However bad the weather, the mountain rescue team is ready to turn out, to seek the needle in the haystack that is one fallen climber on a black mountainside.

Searchlights and helicopters are like manna from heaven for those about to die on a mountainside. They give a very different message to those on the run. The whop-whop-whop of rotor blades in our cities at night, the piercing shaft of the searchlight robbing the suspect of a place to hide, provide an all-too-frequent reminder of a different kind of search.

Sometimes we must seek out to confront and control that which would destabilize our communities and destroy that which we hold most dear in our culture and civilization. Seeking out and finding is not just a case of inexpressible relief, emotional reunions, the best robe and the fatted calf. Seeking out can be an extremely painful duty, informing the next of kin of the sudden death of a loved one, confronting the suspected embezzler of parish funds or abuser of children, challenging an inappropriate friendship that is destroying other people's lives.

Faithfulness in searching will mean acceptance of the burden of both forms of seeking out. The parish priest who evades the responsibility of pointing a flashlight at the darker corners of the life of the community of faith is not likely to be the one who will be first there in the early hours to search with an anxious parent for a missing child.

Of course, our kind of seeking out will not often involve helicopters, searchlights and sniffer dogs. The tools of our trade are empathy and attentiveness and discernment. As we grow as pastors in experience and, we hope, wisdom, we develop by God's grace the skill to get alongside others, to read troubled or confused minds, and to hear silent or muffled cries for help. In our searching we find those who are searching for God.

We learn to distinguish between blather and genuine need, and we come to appreciate the privilege of our calling in being admitted to the heart of people's lives, where all pretence fades and there remains only spiritual nakedness. In that nakedness we encounter the readiness to say 'yes' to God; to hurry down from the tree where we perch ourselves, to welcome God into our lives.

Joe Simpson, that extraordinary climber with nine lives, and hero of the unbelievable survival story *Touching the Void*, leaves little to the imagination in his rejection of the career of mountain guide to which friends kept pointing him. Not for him the pedestrian plodding of those who merely assisted others to climb. His remarks about these 'self-important certificate holders' are mostly unprintable.

While the life of a guide may not appeal to the *prima donnas* of the rock face, for the faithful priest and pastor it will be her heart's desire. For the true guide delights in introducing others to the wonders of mountain climbing, and bursts with a desire to share with others paths trodden in the high hills that are mystical in their power and beauty. More aware than most of the dangers involved, they are trained to lead others safely through the risk-taking, that life may become more intense, more full, more sharply defined than ever before.

The presbyter of the Church of God is above all a true guide, a master of the craft who is content to let others grab the headlines. As true guide, the pastor introduces others to the glimpses of God's glory already known, and safely steers his charges through the risk-taking expeditions into unknown territory that are part and parcel of the adventure of faith.

Searching and guiding . . . what finer calling could there possibly be?

7

DECLARING FORGIVENESS

Formed by the Word, they are to call their hearers to
repentance and to declare in Christ's name the absolution and
forgiveness of their sins.

Authorized Text of the Ordination Services

But while he was still far off, his father saw him and was filled
with compassion; he ran and put his arms around him and
kissed him.

Luke 15.20

None of us are strangers to the need for forgiveness.
There are times in our lives when it becomes the only

thing that matters to us. When we have wronged a person we love, when we have disappointed a person whose approval or good opinion means everything to us, we are desolate until we have put things right. We can think of nothing else but putting the record straight, getting back to where we were; restoring friendship, making peace.

Forgiveness of self is perhaps the most elusive prize of all. The clever but cruel remark that we instantly regret, the broken promise, the missed opportunity, the unspoken word, the relationship entered into impetuously and withdrawn from hurtfully, the impulsive self-centred decision that impacted the lives of so many others, the lost options, the spent life. Remorse is relentless and merciless.

In the wee small hours of the morning, not in a Manhattan bar with Frank Sinatra but alone in bed incapable of sleep, self-recrimination can well up from nowhere and drown us in a sea of hopelessness. We are robbed of peace and of purpose.

It is, of course, the forgiveness of God that alone will rescue and save us. Only through experiencing the mercy of God can we come to forgive ourselves. And this is God the merciful One, revealed to us through the story-telling of Jesus as a loving father who runs across the street to welcome us home, dodging the traffic, smiling and waving.

The route home, the window at which we obtain the free travel voucher to wholeness and peace of mind, is the Church's sacrament of reconciliation. No work which a presbyter of the Church of God will be called upon to do will be as serious and solid, as lasting and life-giving as the solemn declaration of forgiveness in the context of this sacrament. Here the overwhelming grace of God is made tangible and effective; here we witness healing and new life.

In all this, sisters and brothers, you are to be agents of transformation, midwives of a new birthing in the Spirit. How awesome is this place of healing and new beginning; how incredible the part we are called to play in it. 'We declare to you what was from the beginning, what we have heard, what we have seen with our eyes, what we have looked at and touched with our hands, concerning the word of life' (1 John 1.1).

In this sacrament as nowhere else is the role of the presbyter as go-between, as faithful and reliable messenger, brought home to us. We are true friends to the troubled penitent, whose fears we calm and whose hands we take in ours. Yet more wondrous still, we become, in ministering this sacrament, true friends of God, for in this encounter we are admitted to our own 'tent of meeting' in which God speaks to us as he did to Moses 'face to face, as one speaks to a friend' (Ex. 33.11).

We thank God that in our Anglican tradition, this encounter between friends is embodied in our approach to the sacrament of reconciliation, even down to the detail of how we arrange the furniture. We treasure openness, and encounter between friends. Not for us boxes and grills and thick curtains, the visual language of secrecy and grim foreboding.

Instead, confessor and penitent meet as fellow-pilgrims, not judge and accused. Perhaps one will sit and one kneel, or both sit together. They meet out in the open, in full view of anyone else in the church building. There is nothing to hide, for here the grace of God is breaking into our brokenness, and the angels sing.

In my own journey I did not discover this sacrament until university days when, one dark Ash Wednesday evening in Newcastle Cathedral, with knocking knees, parched lips and wobbly intestines, I dragged myself forward to the place of encounter, and stumbled upon the tender loving mercy of God, for me.

Being back in my home parish for Holy Week, I sought out my parish priest to be blessed in this sacrament again. He demurred, never having experienced the sacrament for himself, but being a person of integrity, he asked to borrow the booklet that had helped my own understanding and preparation. He then not only heard my confession, but later wrote to tell me that in due course he had made his own confession too. I have never forgotten his graciousness, nor his modelling for me the enquiring mind, the seeking pilgrim.

Forgiveness is, of course, a funny old thing. Like love, forgiveness can be both used and abused. The sacrament of reconciliation is most clearly abused when we approach it as we would a soft drinks machine, coins ready in our hands.

I am haunted still by tales heard when I was newly ordained, of a clergy house in another diocese where, on Saturday nights, a purple stole was draped in readiness over the banisters on the upper floor. As soon as one of the 'young fathers' came staggering in from a night of debauchery, he would receive from a fellow curate an instant on-the-spot absolution so that he could proceed to the altar the next morning. This little charade was obviously incredibly convenient, but a complete waste of time, not to mention an affront to God.

Forgiveness is also a very complex thing, even when entered into with a generous spirit. Those called to declare God's forgiveness and to minister absolution need to beseech God for discernment, humility and courage. There is no more wondrous place than the confessor's chair, and yet at the same time no tougher spot.

A bishop I once served under asserted that forgiveness is nothing at all unless it means the best robe, the ring and the fatted calf. I was inspired by his words, but he applied them in the context of instituting to a new cure a priest who had been sent packing from another diocese for adulterous behaviour.

Was the bishop's giving him a second chance generous or irresponsible? Was the bishop being fair to the parish to which he was sending this priest? What would the parish have said if the offence concerned not other men's wives, but other people's children?

All we can say is that in the sacrament of reconciliation, the priest, as well as speaking in God's name, represents the whole community of faith. Although the sacramental encounter takes place in utter confidentiality, present around the confessional (at least in the mind's eye of the confessor) stands the assembly of the faithful. Confession in the context of communal life was in the beginning the gold standard of repentance (James 5.16). Although the Church shrank from this with the passage of time, forgiveness must never partake of the character of a cosy deal between a shady politician and a generous contributor to party funds. Instead it must have in itself total integrity, and bear scrutiny before God, whether whispered in secret or shouted from the housetops.

Before we declare in Christ's name the absolution and forgiveness of sins we first have to issue the *call to repentance*. This is no easy task in western society today, where affirmation and personal fulfilment reign supreme, or even in the Church with our new-found emphasis on resurrection rather than the cross. The 'good old days' when preachers at the market cross could in ten minutes gather a crowd and whip them up into a frenzy of weeping and wailing at the enormity of their sins have long since gone.

All we can do is to be ruthlessly, but lovingly, realistic about human nature – our own and everyone else's. We are so crafty and self-delusional that the tricks we get up to in evading-God escapades would be hilarious if they were not so sad. Ever since we romped naked in the Garden we have been busy fooling ourselves about our relationships with one another and with God. Nothing has changed; we've just got bigger wardrobes and fancier clothes with which to continue our cover-up.

Sin is always with us, and therefore the need for presbyters of the Church of God as healers and reconcilers will be with us till the end of time also. It is vital that we are faithful in the call to repentance, and in the bold declaration of the healing power of God. This declaration is not mumbled or half-hearted, but exultant and strong, for these are life-giving words.

In the story of the Good Samaritan (Luke 10.29–37) priests don't get a good press. Now is our chance to make up for the priest and the Levite who went scurrying by. In contrast, let us see our own calling as presbyters of the Church of God as companions of the outcast, and the endangered.

We walk with the stranger on the road going down to Jericho from Jerusalem and wait, knowing full well that sooner or later there will be trouble – there always is. But we are the ones ready with the bandages, the oil and the wine, and with the courage to act. We know how life is, but we have also had given into our hands the healing balm by which God's tender love is released into the bloodstream of humankind.

8

MAKING DISCIPLES

With all God's people they are to tell the story of God's love.
They are to baptize new disciples in the name of the Father,
the Son and Holy Spirit, and to walk with them in the way of
Christ, nurturing them in the faith.

Authorized Text of the Ordination Services

One of the two who heard John speak and followed him was
Andrew, Simon Peter's brother. He first found his brother
Simon and said to him, 'We have found the Messiah' (which
is translated Anointed). He brought Simon to Jesus.

John 1.40–42

For me, Tanzania will always be the one that got away. At theological college we enjoyed a procession of visiting speakers who came to broaden our vision of all that was going on in God's world. One such was a priest who worked among the Masai people of Tanzania. His name has long since gone from my recall capability, but not his presence. He filled the room with the energy of his love for God and for these simple and poor, yet happy and godly people.

I suppose he was slightly crazy, as all the most interesting people are, but whatever else he was he was a maker of disciples. Such was his passion for God, for the work he had been given to do, that I wanted to be around him, work alongside him, offering whatever I had – my five loaves and two fish – that he might use to further the kingdom.

And what did he do? He simply told stories and set the scene, which is exactly what Jesus did. He was on fire with his story, and he made it sound exciting, and dramatic, and ever-changing to be where he was, but also fun, and endlessly fascinating. The end result of all that was that he had the ability to prompt others to stop what they were doing, to listen attentively, to engage, and to change the course of their lives. When people meet a maker of disciples, they leave fishing nets where they are, and abandon boats and even fathers. They even leave bodies unburied, and loved ones are left standing, gaping in astonishment at the lack of even a goodbye.

We, then, as presbyters of the Church of God, must become story-tellers and scene-setters of God's domain. We must speak as travellers from a foreign land where things are different, where everything is possible, a place to which the listener can also journey. We too need to be passionate about the place where we belong in God's scheme of things, and speak with an urgency in encouraging others to come with us to explore it alongside us and help chart its vastness.

Take heart, however; not everyone is a gung-ho missionary on furlough. Other disciple-makers are equally effective through an altogether quieter and gentler approach exercised over a long period of time. This approach is more process than event, but like water running over rock, can make deep inroads into our defences over time.

At the feet of those gentle guides of our formative years – grandparents, teachers, priests – we learned about integrity and sincerity, and about faith as exploration. What was true, what was real? With such people we learned our values and set our sights.

Both the charismatic and the gentle shepherds were effective in making disciples because they were modelling in their own persons the calling of the disciple. They didn't have to say all that much; they just had to be themselves, intensely and totally. Because they each gave their all to God, God could do the rest. They were living, talking billboards for the domain of God.

In one important respect the new Ordinal has taken a backward step. Whereas the Alternative Service Book bids those to be ordained, quite naturally, to go and 'make disciples', now they are permitted only to 'baptize new disciples' (which they presumably have just found conveniently growing on nearby trees). Calvinism, it seems, is not dead yet.

The time-honoured Anglican emphasis on partnership with God (not for nothing was Pelagius one of ours) is discarded in a moment of angst-ridden unworthiness. I bid you ignore it. If we are not here to make disciples, we might as well return to the life we knew before the selection conference and the ordination exam.

The Ordinal does, however, here rightly remind us that we need to complete the process of disciple-making in baptism, emphasizing that we are not primarily in the business of creating individual followers of Jesus who knock around the world in no relationship with one another. Rather, we are in the business of incorporation.

Baptism has always been the natural culmination of the disciple-making process, for in this sacrament we are tumbled into the ragtag and bobtail collection of humanity we call the Church. In our rediscovery of baptism (rather than ordination) as the primary sacrament of Christian identity and ministry, new texts of the Church's worship celebrate the primacy of the baptismal covenant, and new liturgical spaces are now adorned with elaborate and ever-flowing baptismal fonts worthy of a people of God no longer frightened of getting wet.

All this is wholly admirable, and yet there is an unavoidable question mark that needs to be inserted, albeit with some diffidence, about the place of baptism in the context of our disciple-making today.

The way in which we invite people at our Sunday liturgy to the table of the Lord is a fork in the road. It will reveal all. When I was first ordained it was simple; only those confirmed could be admitted to communion. Gradually this was amended to the baptized. Now we would go further. If the most radical thing that Jesus did was to engage in outrageous, unconditional hospitality, enjoying table fellowship with the untouchables of his day, who are we to hedge about with restricted admission to the meal that honours his presence?

The Anglican parish of St Gregory of Nyssa, San Francisco, spells out the alternative option in the layout of its building. At St Gregory's, the font (traditionally placed at the entrance) is located in the garden, beyond the glass doors of the indoor liturgical space. On entering the building our first sight is, therefore, of the altar table, spread ready for the feast of God's people. The building is reminding us that in the natural order of things hospitality comes first, questions about identity and intention and incorporation second.

In our new, post-9/11 world, a further dimension must be added to our questions about baptism. The story of our neighbour in Yorkshire illustrates the dilemma.

Our close neighbour in Huddersfield was a Sikh woman who was daily in the gurdwara, her impoverished home was decorated mainly with pictures of Guru Nanak and other saints of her tradition. Consigned by an arranged marriage to live with a man who was mentally unstable and violent, and speaking hardly any English, she was nevertheless unfailingly cheerful and gracious. Above all, she knew how to smile, and she lived to give. I called her one of the most Christ-like people I had ever met.

She was often in the parish church, for she was at home with God anywhere, and one day, long after I had left the parish, someone went and baptized her. End of a good story.

I am left with the feeling that this wasn't what Our Lord was after. This wasn't necessarily the kind of disciple-making to which we are called. Her grasp of English was so slight that I doubt that even today she is much aware of what she has undertaken, and she is now caught between two cultures and two worlds, unnecessarily compromised in both.

If disciple-making is, rather than clocking up converts, the affirmation of Christ-likeness wherever we find it, then we can safely leave the disciple where we find them, even in the gurdwara.

Andrew's excited cry to his brother Simon, 'We have found the Messiah!' (John 1.41) sprang from his joy from discovering the person who made sense of everything, who in himself provided the missing piece of the puzzle of life. Jesus emerged from the Jewish milieu, but what he brought was not restricted to them. The followers of Jesus constructed an institution around him, but what he brought is not restricted to us either.

Jesus spoke to, and for, all humanity, but he was no imperialist. In his encounters with those outside his own tradition he spoke never of conversion from one label to another, but only of God's irresistible force of love, breaking out anywhere and everywhere. 'You tell me your beautiful names for God, and I'll tell you mine',[1] might well have been his words to the woman at the well.

If we live in this knowledge, proclaiming and being good news without recourse to institutionalism or limitation, will we be so 'charged with the grandeur of God' that we will make disciples everywhere we go, even when we are least aware of doing so. If we tell our story and listen well, we shall be the kind of people worth knowing and worth following. For we shall be unable to stop telling (and hearing) the story of God's love, and of God's domain which is just too wonderful to be the one that got away.

Note

1 C. F. Andrews quoted by Nicholas Holtam, *The Guardian*, 24 December 2005.

9

UNFOLDING THE SCRIPTURES

They are to unfold the scriptures, to preach the word in season and out of season, and to declare the mighty acts of God.

Authorized Text of the Ordination Services

Therefore every scribe who has been trained for the kingdom of heaven is like the master of a household who brings out of his treasure what is new and what is old.

Matthew 13.52

'Unfolding the scriptures' has a beautiful ring to it. I picture someone gently opening the pages of a very old scrapbook. It's a family treasure full of irreplaceable keepsakes; press cuttings yellow with age, a telegram or two (remember those?), an invitation to a swanky dinner, a graduation programme. Folded between the pages lurk other precious things – a pressed leaf or flower, a piece of ribbon, a scribbled note, a love letter.

The scriptures are the scrapbook of the Judeo-Christian family: our treasured repository of the stories and shared memories that make us who we are. Out from its hallowed and well-thumbed pages tumble not just the official line but all the little asides and keepsakes that remind us of the colourful and roguish characters we have in our family history, and the incredible story of our journey.

Note the plural: 'scriptures'. The word 'scripture' suggests a single unified message from Genesis to Revelation. It requires us to believe that God keeps a fax machine in his office from which, through the ages, pages of the good book have fluttered down from the heavens into the hands of God's agents, who simply collected these sheets into a ring-binder labelled 'The Holy Bible'.

Instead, the use of the word 'scriptures' reminds us that the Bible is a library put together under the inspiration of the Spirit by a whole host of recorders and interpreters. Within it are many books and many voices.

Some of these scribes were so self-effacing that we discern the voice of God clearly and with power. Others were so caught up with their own agenda that God is lucky to get a word in edgeways.

Before our increasing knowledge about the way in which this sacred library was put together, blind assertions such as 'the Bible teaches' or 'the Bible tells me so' become less and less tenable. When we unfold the scriptures, therefore, we thank God for that little 's'.

The scriptures are not, of course, just for our pleasure or edification alone. They are the mine from which we dig the gems that will sparkle in the Sunday assembly and will linger in our memory as we journey through the week. The scriptures are the richest resource we have chronicling humankind's endless search for meaning and for God. Prophets, poets, soldiers, buccaneers, lovers and sages have all poured themselves out onto paper, that we may know of God's revelation to them, and thereby may be encouraged and emboldened to continue the search and the journey across the desert.

It is good that we remember constantly the journey, as for me preaching is primarily the provision of 'travel notes': commentary on the route we have taken together. Like a good tour guide, we explain where we are going, give warning of bumps ahead, and point out stunning views or matters of historical interest along the way.

Primarily such travel commentary concerns the journey of the Sunday liturgy itself. If fixed pews and other furniture jammed into our worship space render the notion of journey entirely cerebral, then it's time for the axes and hammers. Journey we must, or lose sight of what we are about as the pilgrim people of God. This is why we need liturgical preaching, not learned treatises on some arcane aspect of the day's gospel.

The journey that the liturgy should be needs continually to be explained, and the components of the liturgy unravelled and examined, so that we may remember who we are and where we are going. The people of God need to be recalled to our journey, for we are a troublesome crew, always longing for the good old days amid the cucumber fields of Egypt. If the notion of liturgical journey surprises us, that means we have become sedentary in our pew for too long, and that it has been far too long since we heard a homily explaining what we are about.

Travel commentary also goes beyond the liturgy to the journey of life, and our world today has more than enough wilderness experience to make the connection irrefutable. We are on a hard road, and the Sunday homily needs to provide packed lunches for the week, rations for daily living.

There is a lot of hullabaloo about preaching, presumably to create a smokescreen to obscure the fact that we are not very good at it. I hear much talk among clergy of the time set apart for sermon preparation (more often on the American side of the pond, I have to say), and my heart sinks when I see preachers with a wad of closely typed sheets in their hands. What have we here? An essay? A dissertation?

What the people of God are hungry for in the Sunday assembly is not a learned study paper, but food (and fire) for the belly. They have a hell of a week coming up, and they are desperate to know how this church lark, these scriptures, this gathering, has any relevance to daily living. To provide such basic food, such iron rations, we may be best advised to throw away our notes altogether, and shoot from the hip.

Bishop Michael Marshall tells the story of how in his own curacy the parish priest would allocate liturgical tasks in the sacristy immediately before Mass, and this included the homily. Such a challenge would reduce many clergy today to a quivering heap, but there it is staring us in the face: 'Always be ready to make your defence to anyone who demands from you an accounting of the hope that is in you' (1 Peter 3.15).

This does not mean that we are henceforth excused preparation time, but it will be spent as much in prayer as in study. Nor does it mean that our preaching is devoid of intellectual content, but it will be part of us, rather than being mugged up from a textbook in a couple of hours. In other words it will take more out of us, not less, but the people will be fed. We may have to practise this new skill in the shallow end, for example at a weekday eucharist, but learn to swim we must, or get a job on dry land.

To be fair to the quiverers, however, our nervousness probably arises because we have allowed preaching as proclamation of good news to be morphed into preaching as academic presentation. This is, of course, useful in many ways. It blunts the gospel as a challenging, converting, transforming power in our daily lives, and it also diverts our attention from what liturgy really is. We can sit back in our boxed or padded pew and forget for a moment that we are called to get off our backsides and follow this crazy guy from Nazareth.

The challenging question that every preacher should ask in concluding preparation of what he or she wants to say is simply this: 'So what?' In other words, will the hearer at the end of the homily be moved to silence, to repentance, to have fresh hope, to try something new? Or will they merely say: 'Very interesting I am sure, but . . . so what?' Where does this take me, lead me? What have I been given that I can hang on to? How might my life be changed?

Such transformation is all the more likely if the proclamation of good news concerns 'the mighty acts of God' rather than stories about ourselves, 'For we do not proclaim ourselves; we proclaim Jesus Christ as Lord and ourselves as your slaves for Jesus' sake' (2 Cor. 4.5). Anecdotes from our own story – especially of the self-deprecating kind – can illuminate and sharpen our message and help identify us with our hearers. But whenever we use that device, there rapidly comes a point – and this means seconds rather than minutes – when we have to switch off ourselves and focus on the One whose messenger we are: 'because our message of the gospel came to you not in word only, but also in power and in the Holy Spirit' (1 Thess. 1.5).

To preach in power does not mean that the syllabus of theological colleges should now include training on how to 'tread on snakes and scorpions' as did the seventy with impunity (Luke 10.19), but it does mean that we preach as if we believed that something was going to happen; that in some real and tangible way the people of God in assembly with us as coach and guide will glimpse the breaking in of the kingdom of God.

Our preaching is not to be at our convenience or the convenience of our hearers, but 'in season and out of season'. People sometimes loiter at the eight o'clock early service because they imagine they will avoid a sermon. Surprise them with a homiletic left hook! There is no close season for preaching, and no protected species of Christian exempt from being exposed to the proclamation of good news with power. Often we shall stumble upon preaching that changes our lives, not in the grand set piece, but at the least expected moment, and the most unlikely place.

R. S. Thomas describes it beautifully in his poem 'The Chapel', in which he speaks of how, before a tiny congregation gathered one evening long ago, in this now near-derelict building,

a preacher caught fire
and burned steadily before them
with a strange light.

Pray that we may so live in the Spirit that we too from time to time may catch fire, and burn for a moment with the brightness of God, warming to life the human heart.

10

PRESIDING AND LEADING

They are to preside at the Lord's table and lead his people in
worship, offering with them a spiritual sacrifice of praise and
thanksgiving. They are to bless the people in God's name.

Authorized Text of the Ordination Services

Let the word of Christ dwell in you richly; teach and
admonish one another in all wisdom; and with gratitude in
your hearts sing psalms, hymns, and spiritual songs to God.

Colossians 3.16

Presiding at the Lord's table on the Lord's day is simply
wondrous, and it should give us stage fright every single

Sunday of our priestly life. I shall never forget how
Father Beasley-Robinson, of the Cowley Fathers, would,
after saying Mass, spend several minutes in the sacristy
gazing in humility and wonder at his hands which 'holy
things had taken'. For us the altar table should always
remain what it was for St John Chrysostom: 'a place of
awe and shuddering'.

'Presiding' is a good word for the role of the presbyter
at the altar table. It may be sniggered at now and then
by those who would have us return to the good old
days when a priest was described as 'celebrating' the
eucharist, but in theological terms 'presiding' is unassail-
able.

'Celebrating' in reference to the chief minister of the
eucharist simply will not do because the whole assembly
of God's people gathered before the Lord's table is a
community of celebrants. Together we con-celebrate or
co-celebrate the eucharistic offering. By contrast, 'presiding' well describes the special calling of the ordained
leader to orchestrate the celebration of the community of
faith. The president or presider gathers and co-ordinates
the celebrants.

It is no accident that in the founding of the Episcopal
Church of the United States as an autonomous church
within the Anglican Communion, the term 'presiding
bishop' was preferred to that of 'archbishop' in desig-

nating its chief pastor. Whereas 'archbishop' retains overtones of medieval prince bishops, 'presiding bishop' has a gentler, less authoritarian ring to it, conveying more accurately the sense of *primus inter pares* so characteristic of the Anglican understanding of leadership.

When we preside, we take the chair, attempting to see fair play and to ensure balance, in order that the outcome of our deliberations does justice to the process of decision-making and reflects the mood of the meeting. Someone who presides does not lord it over the other participants. Indeed, the views of the chair may never be known unless a casting vote is called for, a situation that chairs usually prefer to avoid.

Presiding at the Lord's table is therefore the supreme privilege of the presbyters of the Church precisely because it is our delight to bring forth and to draw out the gifts and ministries of the assembly to produce a paean of praise and thanksgiving to our gracious God. We have relinquished the position of the one-man-band who strove to play the harmonica at the same time as the cymbals and the big bass drum strapped to his back.

Instead we have been enrolled by the Spirit in the masterclass of conducting. We now have a whole orchestra at our disposal. They may be a mixed bag, but each in their own special way will be able to play their part with particular and unsuspected skill, many of them in ways that will leave us standing. To the conductor is given the incredible gift of bringing forth from all these individuals a co-ordinated, harmonious, glorious sound. Herein is our duty and joy as conductors of the eucharistic assembly, presiding over God's sometimes unruly but always surprising band.

It is not enough for the conductor to know what notes come next. Above all, he or she must have a superb sense of rhythm. Timing is everything. The president of the eucharist must also have rhythm, and an impeccable sense of timing.

The eucharistic action has a music of its own, with its own shape and rhythm. The components of the eucharistic action need to be carefully balanced. If the preacher loses the final page of his notes and makes up several more to compensate, or if the leader of the Prayers of the People gives an extended treatise on the current political situation, or if the sharing of the peace becomes a class reunion, then the eucharist will be bent out of shape, and we shall lose the thread of its tune.

To maintain the rhythm of the piece, the conductor will sometimes need to tap her baton on the rail of the rostrum. At times the call is for absolute silence, at others for a quickening of the pace: that movement has taken long enough; on with the next! He will need to slow down and calm the orchestra when they get jittery and in their anxiety rush forward at too fast a pace. Every individual will have a part to play, but the final effect will be harmonious only if everyone watches for their entry and their conclusion.

The president alone (for even the minister of music has to watch the president's beat) will have in her hands the whole shape of the eucharist, producing for God's glory a balanced and beautifully crafted piece of liturgical music.

The conductor must also look the part, by his manner and bearing commanding attention, not easily mistaken for someone in the second row of the first violins. He will do so in a way that draws out from the orchestra respect and affection, a desire to do its very best, rather than a grudging acceptance. The president of the eucharist needs to look as though she knows what she is doing, dressed in a way that distinguishes the president's role but evinces a longing within the assembly to play its part to the very best of its ability.

Vestments are useful things, because they allow the presbyter to decrease that Christ may increase. The president should look the part, like someone *au fait* with things liturgical, rather than someone dressed up at short notice for a part in the village pantomime that is unfamiliar to them.

We need to take some trouble with kitting ourselves

out with vestments that fit, and with which we feel comfortable and fully ourselves. The alb should be long, thus covering a multitude of sins. Girdles and cords around the alb are best avoided, thereby outwitting middle-aged spread and lessening the chance of us appearing like a sack of potatoes tied up with string. The stole and/or chasuble should depend for its impact on colour only, not on intricacy of design or multiplicity of symbols appliquéd onto it.

The president is there not to impose upon the assembly his own life story, as told by the embroiderer, but to play down his person that his office may be recognized and appreciated. The president of the assembly, by virtue of her office, and aided by familiarity with the role, skill born of experience, a loving heart, and wisdom gathered along the way, will be enabled to elicit from her fellow-pilgrims an offering of their very best.

To preside at the Lord's table with style and grace is no easy thing. For some presbyters it is as natural as breathing, for others (the kind who sit in the sanctuary with legs crossed, or pray or read with hands in pockets) it is an uphill struggle. For those addicted to a clod-hopping, bull-in-a-china-shop style of liturgical leadership there is not much hope, until the addict admits the need for help. If he just doesn't get it, there's not much that can be done, and consequently the 'spiritual sacrifice of praise and thanksgiving' of the assembly will be diminished, and its members deprived.

Conversely, when the president of the eucharist has that indefinable gift called 'presence' – the ability to invoke the presence of God by her own attentiveness, bearing, gesture, and voice – then the whole assembly is uplifted by a sense of having been in the company of a friend of God.

At the end of the First Mass of a new priest it is customary for those present to come individually to receive a blessing from the newly ordained. It is a deeply moving moment in the liturgy precisely because of the importance attached from the beginning of recorded time to the blessing by a spiritual or familial elder.

The crime of that devious usurper Jacob (and his scheming mother Rebekah) in cheating his brother Esau of their father's final blessing and bestowal of authority (Gen. 27.1–40) has stayed with us down the years as the quintessential dastardly deed. How *could* a person be such a cad and a bounder (and how come God seems to favour such crooks)? Here we clearly see at work the innate Jewishness of the Christian tradition that sprang from it; somehow we sense that to bless is power, and to deprive another of blessing is about as low as one can stoop. Perhaps the depriving another of blessing comes very close indeed to that 'blasphemy against the Holy Spirit' (Matt. 12.31) that cannot be forgiven.

In contemporary society blessing is both given and received with easy familiarity. 'Have a blessed day' is how a huge proportion of people in the USA will end the recorded greeting on their answerphone. We want to feel blessed, and to bless others, though there remains an ambivalence about blessing in God's name lest we usurp the place of another whose designated role this is. Deep down in our folk memory we know it to be a precious thing, a priestly thing.

In most societies the role of solemnly blessing in God's name is reserved to the holy man or woman to whom we entrust the guardianship of God's ritual presence. It is an awesome privilege and responsibility, and it is ours.

11

SUPPORTING AND DEFENDING

They are to resist evil, support the weak, defend the poor, and
intercede for all in need. They are to minister to the sick and
prepare the dying for their death.

Authorized Text of the Ordination Services

He went to him and bandaged his wounds, having poured oil
and wine on them. Then he put him on his own animal,
brought him to an inn, and took care of him.

Luke 10.34

My grandfather Harry was in retirement an avid gar-
dener, as well as a maker of contraptions and collector of

all manner of things that 'might come in handy one day'. Although a greenhouse remained beyond his means, he had somewhere come upon an old cold frame – a large box with wooden sides and a sliding glass lid – which with delight he re-erected in his back garden, replacing broken panes and giving the sides a lick of paint.

Here in the cold frame he nurtured his seedlings in the delicate early stages of growth, and later in the season forced the more vulnerable or capricious vegetables into early fruitfulness. What Gramp was also doing was living out a parable – although he would never for a moment have thought in these terms – of the way in which he was loving and nurturing and forcing me, his oversensitive and shy grandson, into growth and usefulness.

Presbyters of the Church of God are called to create the conditions – often out of nowhere – in which those young or precarious in the way of faith can be given the protection, warmth and light necessary for growth. We do a bit of 'forcing', too, speeding up the process by which the best is brought out of us at an early stage, and maturity and fruitfulness reached with fewer tears and less wasted time.

'Supporting the weak and defending the poor' will also involve us in much propping up. There is frequent lending of an arm to the unsteady, a great deal of helping the frail or the vulnerable across busy roads in life's journey, some cobbling together of pairs of crutches for periods of intensive recuperation. All this is part and parcel of the presbyter's lot, but the scary part of our calling is that there will also be times for removing the supports and the props: a time for providing crutches and a time for kicking crutches away.

The discarded crutches and other items of dependence that hang in the caves of healing springs and miraculous waters the world over are powerful tokens of the liberation experienced in healing. The presbyter is he who sets before the afflicted and world-weary the very possibility of healing, who books the coach to the shrine where 'prayer has been valid', who helps them down to the pool when the waters are troubled.

My friend Jack, who grew up in a tough fishing community in north-east Scotland, once related how as a boy he nearly came to grief rescuing the minister's son from a gang of bullies. In defending the weak, Jack was doing a priestly thing. Hopefully we won't be called upon all that often to roll up our sleeves for actual fisticuffs, but whether we defend the poor by interrupting a town hall meeting, or demonstrating on the streets, or entering a no-go area of our parish at night, the same courage will be asked of us.

When we minister to the sick and dying, courage will

also be required of us. We often imagine this is the easy bit. As we write out prayer cards and read the scriptures to the terminally ill, and squeeze the hands of the next of kin while looking deep into their eyes, we imagine we are starring in a Bing Crosby black-and-white movie about priests and nuns. The truth is that the presbyter, when entering the valley of the shadow of death, is called both to console and to challenge, combining the roles of faithful and gentle companion with that of the army sergeant who chucks paratroopers out of the aircraft when their moment to jump has come. It's heart-stopping stuff.

With the sick and dying we are there to affirm that God's love is stronger than death, that there is nothing to fear. At the same time we are preparing them for that leap of faith that is the process of dying. We speak the truth about death when all those around you may be muttering platitudes. We are preparing the patient, the penitent, for the final journey. There comes a time for every human being when we have had enough; let's go.

Presbyters are called to be 'stewards of the holy mysteries of God', and the greatest mystery of all, from the beginning of time, is that of God's activity in the day-to-day events of human life. There is too much evil with us, 'late and soon', for us to be sanguine about God's role as interventionist. And yet, we are brought face to face every day with little miracles of love that defy all odds and expectations. The mystery remains unfathomable, but we stand at the edge of the cloud.

If God is God, we shall always retain our conviction that life comes out of death, good out of evil, on a daily basis. The power of focused prayer and the gift of healing given to the Church is too frequent and too well documented to be dismissed.

At the same time we must never become apostles of false hope, trafficking the empty promise that 'everything's going to be all right'. Even if we mean it in an ontological sense, it will be understood in a 'here-and-now' sense. We must be careful always to speak straight, for false assurance is the cruellest of gifts. Intercessory prayer must never be presented as a cure-all form of treatment. Intercessory prayer is not exercising leverage on the Almighty, but simply, as Michael Ramsey described so well, standing in God's presence with another on our heart.

Our Lord in Gethsemane showed us once and for all that there can be no special deals. It is right for us to cast ourselves, on our own behalf and on behalf of others, on the mercy of God with blood, sweat and tears, but we can engineer nothing. God cannot be summoned, nor God's intervention arranged. What we can affirm with power and joy is that when the worst does happen, we shall never be lost. Instead we shall be underpinned by

God whose love is stronger than death. This under-pinning love is conveyed and made real in the first instance by the ministry of those around us in our beloved community of faith; from thereon in, God is revealed in ever-widening circles of compassion.

We know this full well from our own experience of parenting. When a child begs and cajoles and bargains for his or her first bicycle, we shall give in, eventually, but not without misgiving. We shall give them stern warnings about safety, we shall equip them with a helmet, and for as long as is possible cycle alongside them. But there comes the day when we are called upon to watch them wobble off down the road on their own, our hearts in our mouths. In this relationship freedom is of the essence, no matter what uncertainties and fears and potential danger that unleashes.

In ministering to the sick and dying, presbyters are called to mediate the strong and fearless love of a God who is willing to release us into the world and watch us wobble down the road. A God who, as David Jenkins puts it, 'suffers rather than bashes his way through.'

In our turn we have to learn to watch many a wobbly cyclist whom we have sent forth in God's name, and to live with the mixture of pride and anxiety that such moments call forth. We watch the young person we have nurtured into faith go off to university; our key young family relocate to the other end of the country (or to a parish where nothing is the same for them); our right-hand man slip slowly and inexorably into terminal cancer.

In all these situations we are called to love and let go, and nowhere is this more true or more demanding than in watching a parish that we have laboured in and loved go wobbling off on its own once we have moved on to another post. The Church is littered with clergy who cannot let go, who keep finding excuses to come back for the special funeral or wedding; who maintain pastoral relationships with individuals and wheedle their way into celebrations; who construct for themselves a role of the great guru from afar who will always know what to do.

Sometimes we are driven to distraction by the tales that filter through from our old stomping grounds, but we must hold the line. We know that clergy who act in this unprofessional way have never learned to let go. They have not faced up to the personal cost of nurturing spiritual children.

The nurturing business, the supporting and protecting, and the watching of the wobbling, is incredibly hard work and it drains us. Gramps knew that with his cold frame and with his grandson, and if we are faithful we shall discover every day how hard is the calling to love and let go. We can but give the frame a fresh lick of paint, make good the broken panes, prepare the soil, carefully tend the seedlings, and let it be. It is our business as presbyters to know and to declare that God will do the rest.

12

DISCERNING AND FOSTERING

Guided by the Spirit, they are to discern and foster the gifts of
all God's people, that the whole Church may be built up in
unity and faith.

Authorized Text of the Ordination Services

Now there are varieties of gifts, but the same Spirit; and there
are varieties of services, but the same Lord; and there are
varieties of activities, but it is the same God who activates all
of them in everyone.

1 Corinthians 12.4–6

For polar explorers, edging through the ice pack in
search of open water, an experienced ice pilot was the

key to a ship's survival. *Terra Nova*, the support ship of the 1911 Antarctic expedition of the brave but inept Captain Scott, missed by a hair's breadth being trapped (and thereby crushed to pieces) because it had no one of experience to scour the horizon and steer a path through the pack ice:

> Navigating pack ice, especially off an uncharted coast, is a specialized occupation. There was no ice pilot on board . . . 'Terra Nova' was very nearly beset. After 'dodging about like a rat in a trap' she escaped from the ice, having cut it very, very fine.[1]

Just as the ice pilot is trained to discern a path through uncharted waters of great potential danger, knowing the difference between an iceberg and a cliff, a cloud bank and a distant shore, so the priest discerns for the community of faith the difference between what is illusory and what is real. It is a 'specialized occupation'.

'Discernment of spirits' is a spiritual gift of tremendous importance in building up the Body of Christ (1 Cor. 12.10), for illusion and tricks of light are not restricted to the polar regions. We can deceive ourselves all too easily in the spiritual life, and false prophets can flourish in faith communities as nowhere else. The very generosity of spirit and tolerance that characterizes the Church at its best are easily abused by the charlatan or the deluded religious nutcase. Great harm can be done, and many years wasted.

Illusion surrounds us on all sides. We are bombarded by the advertising industry's propaganda, promoting the 'good life' attainable for just a few hundred pounds more. Our hedonist culture whispers sweet falsehoods in our ear. Like *Terra Nova*, we are very nearly beset. The faithful presbyter, eyes fixed on the horizon, corrects our course towards the things of God.

The priest guides us through the pack ice, searching for the distant leads of open water that will take us to safety, while disregarding the false trails in the foreground. Paul, writing to the church at Corinth, warned of the necessity of 'discerning the body' (1 Cor. 11.29). If we see things only superficially, we fail to recognize the true significance and import of what we are and what we do as the community of faith.

The presbyter is he who discerns the body, seeing things as they really are, calling things by their real name, giving illusion and self-deception short shrift.

It is an extremely lonely role. Priests like Hans Küng who, through recalling the Church to its first love of God was ostracized by his own Communion, remind us what a terrible price may have to be paid by the prophet who discerns things as they really are. We can but pray for such courage.

Expeditions to unforgiving places require a team well balanced in expertise and human relationships. Although the Church is not a body formed through careful screening and selection, it is by the grace of God a community in which all necessary gifts and ministries and expertise will be found. All we need is a faithful priest who will discern those gifts amid the least likely faces and places, and fan the flickering flame of the Spirit within them into life.

In fanning the flames of the Spirit, the presbyter will foster the children of God placed in her care. Fostering children from broken or dysfunctional or even abusive situations is heroic work requiring toughness, patience and perseverance springing from an enormous loving heart.

There are many setbacks on the way in fostering, and frequent failures. But the impact on a young person, plucked from neglect or violence, of being embraced by a loving family in a regular routine, can only be imagined. The cycle of neglect and despair will be broken. What makes the difference is the security and certainty of new relationships. 'Home' and 'family' are no longer words used in an ironic sense, but take on a whole new meaning.

John and Greg Rice were twin brothers who, afflicted with dwarfism, were abandoned in infancy by their mother. Only 2 feet 10 inches tall, they became celebrities in their native Florida: estate agents, TV personalities and community leaders, as much 'a part of Palm Beach County as the palm trees', as one admirer put it on John's death in 2005. How did this happen? Because they were embraced by foster parents who 'raised them with abundant love and gave them confidence, *joie de vivre* and the urge to give back. "Our mom sat us down and told us, 'Yes, you guys are different, but think of yourselves as a couple of dimes in a handful of nickels.'"'[2]

The presbyter is there to make a difference to people's lives. Like that mom, we are called to love people where they are, and how they are, and to transform the way they see themselves and how they look at life. We are foster parents at large, taking under our wing those who are battered or lost and providing for them the security of 'mother Church' – a set of new relationships that make real and tangible the concept of a loving community in which the individual can be cherished and valued. *Joie de vivre* is our stock in trade.

In this community of faith and forgiveness the individual who belonged nowhere, the person without meaning or direction in life, can finally come home, can find purpose and wholeness. For the priest who is a true pastor, it doesn't get much better than that.

In foster families, of course, one doesn't sit around all day feeling cosseted; there is much to be done, from peeling potatoes to learning consideration, and remembering birthdays, and saying sorry. Foster parents are busy watching out for special gifts and skills, encouraging aptitudes here, redirecting energies there, always bringing out the best.

The Church is no different. Priests are parents who are always on the lookout for special gifts and aptitudes among their spiritual charges. They crouch down at the hearth of the Church and breathe new life into the glowing embers of those just starting out on their spiritual journey, or those who are somewhat weary and feel they have nothing left to give. The presbyter of God is proud of those in his care, and delights to bring forth those gifts and ministries that will transform lives and re-energize the Body of Christ.

The gifts and ministries shared among the people of God are not, of course, for our own satisfaction, self-aggrandizement or entertainment, but for beefing up the community's health and effectiveness. 'Since you are eager for spiritual gifts,' says Paul to the church at Corinth, 'strive to excel in them for building up the church' (1 Cor. 14.12). Whether bricks or mortar, or even bits of straw, our proudest boast as the people of God can be merely that, like any sound building, we keep out the rain and provide a place to be, and to become. This boils down to something as simple as dependability.

Showing up, as Woody Allen reminds us, is 90 per cent of the game.

As presbyters we soon come to prize above all other gifts among our flock, that of loyal and patient and self-effacing service of God in the assembly of faith; showing up and asking, 'What do you need? How can I help?' Such qualities are not just preached about by the faithful presbyter, but embodied, enfleshed, made real.

John Fenton writes of the testimony of the author of Mark's Gospel:

> He only wants us to think one thing: Love for God cannot coexist with any other sort of love; it is exclusive in its demands; it is like marriage; there is no place for a bit on the side; all your heart, all your soul, all your mind, all your strength – and all your money too.[3]

That's not a bad description of the life, the priorities and the passion that God wants of us as presbyters of the Church of God. It is no easy task; it demands of us yet another mile when we think we can't go on; we are never finished, we can never rest.

But as the psalmist says, 'weeping may linger for the night, but joy comes with the morning' (Ps. 30.5), and God's love for us really is new every morning, freshly baked. More joy than we could ever have imagined, more than we are ever likely to find elsewhere in this life. To be a parish priest really is the best job in the whole world.

> However, keep the lively taste you hold
>   Of God, love him as now, but fear Him more;
> And in your afternoons think what you told
>   And promised Him at morning prayer before.

John Donne, To Sir Henry Goodyere

Notes

1 Roland Huntford, *The Last Place on Earth*, New York, Atheneum, 1985.
2 *New York Times*, 17 November 2005.
3 John Fenton, *More about Mark*, London, SPCK, 2001.